I Saw Heaven

by
Roberts Liardon

Harrison House
Tulsa, Oklahoma

Unless otherwise indicated, all Scripture quotations are taken from the *King James Version* of the Bible.

13th Printing
Over 136,000 in Print

I Saw Heaven
ISBN 0-89274-820-6
(Formerly ISBN 0-89274-551-7)
Copyright © 1983, 1991 by Roberts Liardon
P.O. Box 30710
Laguna Hills, CA 92654
All Rights Reserved
Printed in U.S.A.

Published by Harrison House, Inc.
P. O. Box 35035
Tulsa, Oklahoma 74153

Foreword

Roberts Liardon is a young man who has matured spiritually far beyond his years. As you read this anointed book, remember that God is no respecter of persons.

As a student in Victory Christian School, Roberts provided a consistent model of Christian character. He was respected by students, teachers, and administrators.

In counseling Roberts early in his ministry, I cautioned him about the danger of pride. Success at such a young age is often spoiled by arrogance. In my estimation, Roberts has been able to handle the rapid progress with God's grace.

You will be blessed as you read to know there is a quality life behind these pages. Jesus truly is reflected in the life of this young man.

Billy Joe Daugherty, Pastor
Victory Christian Center
Tulsa, Oklahoma

Contents

I call to remembrance the unfeigned faith that is in thee, which dwelt first in thy grandmother . . . and thy mother . . . ; and I am persuaded that in thee also.

2 Timothy 1:5

Dedicated to:

My "great and gracious Gram,"
Mrs. Gladoylene Moore,

My parents,
Fred and Carol Liardon, and

My sister, Priscilla Liardon,
"the silent supporter"
of my ministry.

Introduction

A shorter version of this book was published in 1983. Since then, I have had many questions asked me concerning my trip to heaven. I have tried to answer some of those in this book. Other things, I cannot answer — either because the question involves things Jesus will not let me reveal as yet, or because I simply do not know the answer.

The first book was written primarily to believers, and I took for granted readers would know the scriptural basis for certain things that I saw in heaven and that I wrote about in that book.

However, a number of years have gone by since then. In the meantime, thousands of souls have been born into the Kingdom of God who have no background in Bible study. So for their benefit, and for the benefit of the many unbelievers whom, I believe, God intends to read *this* book, I have included the scriptures that apply to what I saw.

The most important thing I can tell any reader is this:

Jesus is a real Person.

He is alive today, walks with those who will receive Him, and will return for all believers still living. He *has* gone on ahead of us to rule and reign over all things and to prepare mansions (John 14:2) for each person who is born again.

I would ask you to read this book with that truth in mind.

If you are already a believer, I pray this will strengthen your faith, encourage your hope, and give you an added expectancy of His soon return.

If you are not a believer, read the story of my visit to heaven. Then, in the last chapter, I have told you how you too can make sure of being in heaven some day. There is no security like that of knowing you are going to spend eternal life with the Creator in a supernatural Kingdom. Your life will have light where now there is darkness.

— Roberts Liardon

1

Young Men Shall See Visions

. . . This is that which was spoken by the prophet Joel; (Joel 2:28-30)

And it shall come to pass in the last days, saith God, I will pour out of my Spirit upon all flesh: and your sons and your daughters shall prophesy, and your young men shall see visions, and your old men shall dream dreams.

And on my servants and on my handmaidens I will pour out in those days of my Spirit: and they shall prophesy.

Acts 2:16-18

I was born in Tulsa, Oklahoma, because my parents moved there for my mother to attend Oral Roberts University. While she was attending ORU, I was born. Since I was the first baby boy born to a student, they named me Kenneth Roberts Liardon.

ORU Founder and President Oral Roberts and his wife, Evelyn, wanted the privilege of helping name the first boy and the first girl to be born to students of the then-new university. I have always been proud of my name because of its origin.

When I was between five and six years of age, my father left and I did not see him again for many years. At that time, my grandmother, an Assembly of God pastor, came to live with us. Grandmother pastored for many years alongside my grandfather. Together, they started more than 20 churches, mainly country Pentecostal congregations, during their ministry.

11

Grandfather had died about four years earlier, so Grandmother came to Tulsa to help raise me and my sister, Priscilla, in order for Mother to finish school and also be able to work to support us.

One of the main things I remember about those years of my childhood is all of the prayer that went on in our house. We had more prayer at home than we did in church! I saw more of the power of God, more healings, more evidence of God in our home than I did at church.

I do not mean that in any derogatory or critical way. I am simply stating facts. I believe these things happened because there was so much awareness of the Lord in our home.

Many times, it seems I talk more about my grandmother in my books and messages than my mother. But there are two reasons for that, neither of which is that my mother was less spiritual, less strong in prayer, or less of an influence than my grandmother.

However, Grandmother spent more time with Priscilla and me than our mother, who was working *and* finishing school. The second reason is that I knew even as a child I was called to preach. Therefore, as Grandmother was a preacher, she spent more time training me.

Her "training" mostly involved prayer and reading the Word. When we had family prayer, my sister and I were not allowed to just sit and listen, and certainly not to watch television or color in coloring books while the grownups prayed!

When it was time to pray, we had to kneel down just as they did. (At that time, many people thought they were not praying if they were not kneeling.) We were not expected to pray all of the time that our mother and grandmother prayed, because sometimes their prayer times would be hours long.

But we were told to pray as much as we could. They knew what our limit of attention span and physical stamina was, and they encouraged us to pray to that point and a little beyond to build endurance in prayer. That is the way they trained us to be able to flow into a long season of prayer or intercession as the Holy Spirit leads.

We prayed in English, and we prayed in tongues. (1 Cor. 14:14,15). Also, we memorized scriptures at home as well as at Sunday school. As we were eating breakfast or going out the door for school, Mother or Grandmother — whoever was getting us off to school that day — would ask us what verse we were memorizing that week. Sometimes, we were memorizing three or four verses.

Some people, who have heard me tell or have read in my books about this kind of upbringing, have received the wrong impression.

Some will say, "Boy, you had a tough childhood!"

No, I did not have a "tough childhood." We lived under a divine discipline that flowed out of the Spirit of the Lord in love and compassion. The spirit of rebellion that permeates the world never had a chance to get hold of us as children. Rebellion was not allowed in our home.

After the divorce, even more prayer began to take place in our home. And, yes, there are things in my life even yet that I have to work through because of the divorce. But, in comparison to many other children of broken homes whom I have met or read about, we have come through quite well, *because* of the prayer and strong emphasis on the Word.

Many times, the Word working in us broke feelings of rejection and self-pity that otherwise might have set up strongholds. Many times, I would get on the school bus and head for school praying under my breath or quoting verses of scripture.

There were times, of course, when I felt badly that I did not have a dad to do things with. There were times other kids would ask me about my dad.

Then I might be wanting to cry and say, "Where is my dad? Where is he when I need him?"

All of a sudden, I would remember my mother and grandmother saying, "You may not have a natural father living with you every day, but you have a heavenly father Who is with you every day. He will be your dad, if you let Him."

And, at one of those moments of remembering what they had said, there was a revelation of truth. The seed they had planted within me began to grow, and I *knew* beyond the shadow of a doubt that knowing my heavenly Father was the most important thing in my life.

My mother remarried when I was about 15, but the Holy Spirit by that time had become my "dad" in many respects.

It was wonderful to have the kind of relationship with God that we had at home. I found at school that, because of the strong principles from the Word that had been placed inside me, I could not use certain words or do certain things the other kids did. Especially during my teenage years, I was out of step with my peers (or better stated, my peers were out of step with God).

I had been taught not to lie, not to steal, not to covet. The Ten Commandments were a way of life. If any of the other children made fun of us, and we came home and told of it, Mother or Grandmother would say: "Truth outlives a lie."

But my sister and I were not unique in receiving some persecution for our way of life. The problem of peer pressure is there for Christian teenagers in any situation or generation. We were able to handle it without bending or breaking because of the love and respect we had developed for our mother and grandmother and for Jesus.

Respect for Elders in the Lord

When I see how many children today have been allowed to operate in disrespect for their parents and older relatives, I often think of the story of the turtle and the rabbit.

Most of you probably remember hearing the story as children:

A rabbit and a turtle set out to run a race. The rabbit, which in this illustration is symbolic of a lie, seems to be gaining in the race. He seems to be a sure winner. It seems the truth, represented by the turtle, will never get to the finish line. The lie is bouncing everywhere with everyone's eyes on it.

However, the rabbit is over-confident, and he decides to take a nap. He thinks he "has it made." While he is resting, the turtle crosses the finish line and wins.

During the past few years, when rumors have run rampant concerning nearly every ministry and well-known minister, I have stood on that principle.

I have said, "They may say this, and they may say that, but the truth will outlive a lie."

The truth is that honoring the elderly, especially elderly ministers — those "elder statesmen" of the faith — will add to your knowledge and to spiritual wisdom. There are many things we can learn from them, just as I learned from my grandmother's long experience in the ministry.

Actually, I come from a long line of preachers, so my grandmother learned from her ancestors and passed it along to me. I am not just talking of the wisdom of one generation. For several generations back, there have been preachers in my family.

There were United Brethren circuit riders, preachers in various denominations, and my grandfather and grandmother, the first Pentecostal preachers in the line.

I am grateful to my mother and grandmother that they insisted on our reading four chapters a day in the Bible in order to finish it in a year, and that they insisted that we pray every day. That is just the way we lived.

And I believe the "turtle" of truth concerning the value of listening to and honoring our parents, grandparents, and those older in the Lord will hit the finish line in this generation. I believe in these endtime-years, we will see a return to this principle and others God has set out in His Word.

We must have an understanding of the continuity between the past, present, and future in order to make a climate for God to do His signs and wonders. Through prayer, spiritual maturity, knowledge of the Word, and learning from the lessons of the Church's past, we will be prepared to walk in the supernatural, as God's Spirit is poured out on all flesh.

Upon *All* Flesh

The Apostle Peter said the prophetic words at the beginning of this chapter began to be fulfilled on the Day of Pentecost. Those words were spoken forth by the Prophet Joel more than 800 years before Christ. The "last days" began at the Day of Pentecost, according to Peter and some of the other writers of the New Testament epistles and books. (Heb. 1:2, 1 Pet. 1:20, 1 John 2:18.)

You can see that Joel listed several characteristics of "the last days" which, in his day, were still to come:

• God would pour out His Spirit on *all* flesh, meaning that everyone would come into contact with the power of the Lord in some way. Unbelievers all over the world are deciding, or will have to decide in this generation, what they are going to do with God.

• A surge of manifestation of God's supernatural power would come on the youth, both male and female.

• The youth would see visions, have supernatural dreams, and prophesy.

As we move closer to the end of this age, I believe visions, dreams, and other operations of the Holy Spirit will come more and more into manifestation. Discernment of supernatural manifestations will be absolutely necessary, as well as testing of doctrines.

Satan always tries to counterfeit what God does. When he sees the Holy Spirit moving in a certain way, he comes up with a duplicate move. Much of what is known as "New Age" counterfeits Bible miracles, signs, and wonders.

As I have traveled around the world in the last decade and studied church history of past years, it has become obvious that more and more Christians are experiencing the fulfillment of Joel's prophecy.

Many believers tell of dreams and visions pertaining to heaven, hell, or spiritual things in books and publications, such as *Guideposts* and the monthly magazine of the Full Gospel Business Men's Fellowship International.

In fact, the Lord promised as early as the days of Moses to make Himself known to His prophets in visions and dreams. (Num. 12:6.) The very first mention of a vision in the Bible is when the Lord came to Abram in a vision and told him to leave Ur of the Chaldees and go to a far country that He would show him. (Gen. 15:1.)

Great men of the day report having had more than one vision.[1]

So, I feel privileged to have been allowed to visit heaven when I was only eight years old. But at the same time, I do not consider myself in any way unique — not in these "last days." And, of course, in Bible days, there were numerous occasions when men of God saw visions and dreamed dreams.

Isaiah saw **the Lord sitting upon a throne, high and lifted up** (Is. 6:1); Ezekiel had a number of visions during his years as a prophet to the Jewish exiles in Babylon, as did Jeremiah, who was prophet to the remnant of Judah left in Jerusalem. Also, after the return from exile, Zechariah saw several visions.

The list of such Biblical experiences would be quite long, if we wrote them all down.

Visions, Dreams, and Supernatural Experiences

We see three kinds of visions described in the Bible, particularly in the Old Testament: spiritual visions, trances, and open visions. In addition, any of the three kinds of visions can be *literal* or *symbolic.*

There are also night visions, or dreams. There are dreams of literal and symbolic things given by the Holy Spirit for various reasons. And there are other supernatural experiences — such as Philip, the disciple of Jesus and early evangelist, being *transported* bodily from one place to another. (Acts 8:39.)

In the Old Testament, Elisha literally *saw* Elijah taken up into a chariot of fire pulled by horses. That was not a

---

[1]Hagin, Kenneth E. I Believe in Visions (Tulsa: Faith Library Publications, Copyright 1988 by Rhema Bible Church).

Publications of Dr. Lester Sumrall and Norvel Hayes are available from Harrison House, Tulsa, Oklahoma 74153.

vision, open or closed (2 Kings 2:11), but was a real occurrence, a time when the supernatural intruded into the natural world.

Apparently, the sons of the prophets waiting for Elisha to return across the river also saw what happened. They assumed that Elijah's spirit went in the chariot without his body, so they insisted on looked for his body for three days, although Elisha told them not to bother. (2 Kings 2:16-18.)

A *spiritual, or closed, vision* is something — a scene, happening, or place — seen with the "eyes of the spirit," not with the natural eyes. The vision, if it is literal, might be of earthly things or of heavenly things.

The Apostle John on the Isle of Patmos saw spiritual (closed) visions, some were literal — such as Jesus standing behind him (Rev. 1:13-16) — and some things were symbolic — such as the seven golden candlesticks (seven churches) among which Jesus was standing, and the two-edged sword in His mouth. We know they were spiritual visions, because John wrote that he was *in the Spirit*. (Rev. 1:10.)

The Apostle Peter's vision of the clean and unclean beasts was a *trance*, so Luke wrote in the Acts of the Apostles. (Acts 11:5.) In his trance, Peter saw a sheet let down by the four corners from heaven containing all kinds of tame and wild beasts, birds, and creeping things. He also heard a voice (Jesus) speak to him from heaven. (Acts 11:7-9.)

Peter saw the same vision three times. This was a vision of *symbolic* things. The interpretation of what he saw was given him by the Lord: **What God hath cleansed, that call not thou common** (Acts 11:9b). Through the context of the rest of chapter 11, we understand that the things he saw were symbolic of the Gentiles (non-Jewish peoples), whom the Jewish nation of that day called "unclean."

God used this *trance* to change the direction of Peter's life and ministry.

The prophet Balaam apparently saw an *open vision* when God opened his eyes to see the angel standing in front of him with a drawn sword. (Num. 22:31.) Balaam's donkey also saw the angel with natural eyes. But when the donkey *spoke* to Balaam (Num. 22:28-30), that was a *supernatural occurrence.*

Apparently, my experience would fall more into the *supernatural occurrence* category than in the categories of visions.

As far as spiritual dreams go, Bible examples include the Pharaoh of Joseph's day, Nebuchadnezzar, and the prophet Daniel. Also, an angel appeared to Joseph, who was betrothed to Mary, mother of Jesus, and warned him of things concerning Jesus at least three times. (Matt. 1:20; 2:13,20.)

Spiritual dreams may be more common today than visions or supernatural occurrences.

There is no way you can *earn* a vision or a trip to heaven. I know nearly every Christian would love to have a preview of heaven or to see Jesus. There seems to be no criteria for these experiences except the sovereign will of God.

I do believe all of the prayers that were prayed over me by my mother and grandmother had a lot to do with it. Also, my heart was open to Jesus, and as far as I know, there was no doubt or disbelief present in my mind at all about the Bible, the Trinity, and heaven and hell.

However, my primary belief is that God's will alone is involved in selecting those people for these experiences. Also, I know it is not because He favors those selected, but their visions, dreams, and experiences are designed to further God's plan in the earth in some way.

Ultimately, I believe He does these things to establish His will and His Kingdom rather than primarily for the benefit of those who see and hear into the supernatural realm. In other words, they are for *His* purposes, not just for our enjoyment.

2
Caught Up to Heaven

In the summer of 1974, when I was eight years old, I went into my bedroom after school one day to read my daily assignment in the Bible. I wanted to hurry up and finish reading the four chapters of the Gospel of John that I was to read that day, so I could get back out and play with my friends.

I lay down on the bed with my Bible in my hands. As soon as my head touched the pillow, however, the Bible, the bed, my room, and even my body disappeared! I had no warning. Suddenly, the real me — the Roberts Liardon who is a spirit being and occupies this body (2 Cor. 5:1-10) — was moving through the heavens at a high rate of speed.

At the time, as a little boy I had no knowledge of the fact that God's Word speaks of more than one heaven. Since then, I have learned that when Genesis 1:1 speaks of God creating **the heavens and the earth,** Bible scholars agree that there are three heavens.

The first heaven is earth's atmosphere, according to Old Testament writings.[1] And the ''second heavens,'' are generally considered to be space and the area where Satan and his demons have lived since being cast out of the third heaven. (Rev. 12:4.) The *third heaven* is the place where God lives, according to scripture.

---

[1]Elwell, Walter A., Editor, *Encyclopedia of the Bible*, Vol. 1 (Grand Rapids: Baker Book House, 1988), pp. 940, 941.

Paul's references to "the heavenlies," or as sometimes translated, *in heavenly places*, all occur in Ephesians:

In Ephesians 1:20,21, he wrote of Christ having been set at God's right hand in the heavenly places **far *above* all principality, and power, and might, and dominion, and every name that is named.**

In Ephesians 3:10, Paul wrote that Jesus intends the Church, His Body, to make known **unto the principalities and powers in heavenly places . . . the manifold wisdom of God.**

And, of course, the Apostle Paul wrote of a man he knew — whom most people believe to be the apostle himself — who was taken out of the body and into *the third heaven* just as I was. (2 Cor. 12:2.)

In the Old Testament, the term "heaven of heavens" (Deut. 10:14; 1 Kings 8:27; Ps. 68:33; 148:4) is considered to parallel Paul's expression, "the third heaven."

All I knew that afternoon in 1974 was that suddenly I was flying through the heavenlies at an unbelievable speed. I passed many things in the first heaven, then zoomed through the second heaven, and landed outside of the biggest gate I had ever seen — or have ever seen since.

All I can say is that it was very wide, very tall and had no cut or blemish in it. This gate was made of one solid pearl, one immense glossy, glowing white pearl, and the edges were carved with a design. It was the biggest gate I had ever seen in my life. Its presence gave forth not an aura — but its own glow — its own life.

I shook myself to see if I were dreaming. It had all happened so fast. But I decided it was real when I heard a voice speaking to me.

A man said, "This is *one* of the gates."

I turned around, and there stood *Jesus Christ in all His glory!* Immediately, I recognized Him, although He did not look like any pictures I had ever seen. All I can say is that, when you are faced with the presence of Jesus, you *know* beyond the shadow of a doubt Who it is.

Many people since have asked me what He looks like. (I have noticed that when anyone tells of having seen Jesus, the first thing other people want to know is, ''What did He look like?'') From my own experience, anyone who sees Jesus is so overwhelmed that His appearance is secondary to His literal presence. You are so caught up in *Who* He is that the details of what He looks like are not what your mind focuses on or retains.

However, I do remember that He looked about six feet tall, with sandy-brown hair, not real short and not too long. The most outstanding impression I retained was that He was a perfect man. The way He looked, talked, and moved was perfect. That is what I remember the most, the impression of perfectness and wholeness.

In the years since this event, when I have talked about heaven, or when people have read my earlier book, many have said to me, ''But Jesus has dark hair.''

Perhaps they are right. Perhaps His hair looked lighter to me because of the light of His presence or the glory about Him. All I know is that it looked sandy-brown. Or perhaps they think His hair is black because of medieval paintings that portray Him that way or because of his being Jewish.

On the other hand, the Apostle John saw Jesus with hair **white like wool, as white as snow** (Rev. 1:14). So I cannot argue about the color of Jesus' hair. I can only relate the way *I* saw it.

I buckled to my knees, and tears began to stream down my face. I could not have stopped them if I had tried. Every time Jesus speaks, it is as if arrows of faith propelled by love shoot into you and explode inside. Your only way of reacting is to weep.

Then He spoke again, "I want to give you a tour through heaven because *I love you so much.*"

And He does not love me anymore than He does you. God is no respecter of persons. (Acts 10:34.) The tears began to pour down my face again.

Jesus said, "Now, no more tears. But a face full of joy would make me glad."

Then he laughed, and I did too. He came over to me, picked me up, and dried away the tears. My tears were not of sadness nor sorrow, nor were they of fear. Again, all I can say is that the presence of Jesus is so tender to your spirit that joy spills over in tears.

We do not have words here on earth (in our earthly vocabularies) to describe Jesus or heaven. All we can do — those who have seen Jesus or heaven — is express what we saw in terms of what it was "like" on earth, and that is a poor picture compared to the real thing.

Life in Heaven

Jesus escorted me through that huge gate. He did not ask anyone to open it, and He did not push a button. The gate just opened up, and we walked through.

The first thing I saw was a street, and it was gold.

As I walked through heaven later, I saw that all of the streets looked as if they were literally made of *pure* gold. Even the curbs were of gold. (Rev. 21:21.) And the curbs were lined with flowers in all colors of the rainbow.

I thought, "If this is heaven, then these *are* gold streets I'm standing on," and I made a mad dash for the curb.

From a distance, I saw that Jesus turned to say something to me, but I was gone.

He looked at me and said, "What are you doing over there?"

I was standing on the grass alongside the curb with eyes and mouth wide open in surprise. I answered Him two words: *golden streets!* Some of the streets looked like gold on earth. That is how I recognized what it was. But other parts of the streets were so transparent that the gold was as clear as crystal.

Jesus laughed and laughed. I thought He was never going to stop. Then He said, "Come over here."

I said, "No, those streets are *gold.* I can't walk on them! (The only time I had seen gold was in rings on people's fingers. I knew it was very expensive and very valuable.)

But Jesus beckoned to me. "Come on," He said. He kept laughing as He walked over to where I was and led me back into the street.

"These streets were made for those who have accepted Me into their hearts. This place is made for my younger brothers and sisters. (Rom. 8:29, John 14:2,3.) You are one of my younger brothers, so enjoy them."

As we walked along, I became aware that the atmosphere of heaven is wonderful because it is energized with the fruits of the Spirit. (Gal. 5:23,24.) The very breezes were filled with the presence of God. Sometimes on earth when you are prayed for by someone ministering under a heavy anointing, your body may break out in goose bumps. But even when the body does not react to the supernatural presence of the Holy Spirit, there is a feeling of inner warmth, of being wrapped in a blanket of God's love. That is the way heaven felt, only more so.

We passed towns, buildings, and little offices. The buildings were for whatever "business" or interaction that takes place in heaven. I saw people coming and going, and they were all smiling. Some sang songs I recognized from earth, and some sang heavenly songs that I had never heard. They carried little bundles, and some of them carried books.

I do not believe there is an exchange of money, but people *were* going in and out of those buildings to get things. I saw a woman walk into one place with a little bundle of goods of some kind and walk out with a book.

There are books and songs in heaven that are intended for our knowledge and enjoyment in praising God on earth. But to my knowledge, no man or woman has yet paid the price to receive them for the benefit of the Body of Christ. For there is a price to pay. You must pay the price to walk in the Spirit and receive inspiration from heaven through the Holy Spirit. You "pay the price" by putting God first, spending much time in prayer, and loving His Word above all earthly pleasures, knowledge, and entertainment.

In the New Testament, the Apostle Paul wrote that there is one family in heaven and earth. (Eph. 3:15.) He did not say there is one family in heaven and another family down here. There is *one* family *in heaven and earth.* I believe there are many things about our "family" that we do not understand as yet.

As we walked on through this section of heaven that really was like a small town, I saw street signs. We came to one that I do not remember the name of, and we turned right on it.

Mansions Are Prepared for Us

As we walked up what looked like an unpaved, dirt path, I saw a gigantic house above the trees. Even now, as a grown man remembering that house, I know that it *was* a mansion. (John 14:2.) This structure did not just look huge because I was a little boy.

Jesus talked to me the whole time we walked up the path toward the house. Jesus is a Person, and you can talk to Him about everyday things. He is our *friend,* as well as a member of the Godhead Who rules and reigns. We do not have to make a visit to heaven to talk to Him, either!

Jesus is with us here on earth. He would never leave us nor forsake us. (Heb. 13:5.)

The Trinity — God, the Father; Jesus, the Son; and the Holy Spirit — have emotions. Otherwise, we would not have emotions, because we were created in their image. (Gen. 1:26.) However, unlike most of us, They are not at the mercy of their emotions. They are not ruled by "feelings." They operate by doing what is right to do, regardless of how they feel. So while we have emotions, we shouldn't be ruled by them.

When someone hurts *our* feelings, we get into self-pity, we get angry, and many times, we retaliate in some way. Jesus can be grieved at our attitudes, but He never changes in the way He loves us or treats us. He has no self-pity, no anger on his own behalf, and no retaliation.

We were not created to operate in negative emotions. Those became part of us when Adam and Eve disobeyed God and had to leave the Garden of Eden. But we ought to be extremely careful not to grieve Jesus, the Holy Spirit, or the Father, because we love them. There is no way we can love them as much as they love us, but we ought to love them as much as possible.

His love permeated everything Jesus said or did with me during my visit. I will never forget the revelation of what love really is.

When we got to the door of this mansion, Jesus walked up and knocked on the door. That is part of love — being considerate of other people's feelings, time, and privacy. People in heaven were very polite.

We waited about three minutes, and then He knocked again, before anyone ever came to the door. Then a little gentleman opened the door, stuck his head out, and spoke to us. I did not see anyone just "floating through the walls."

He said, "How are you doing, Jesus? And how are *you* doing, Roberts?"

I almost took off running. That man knew my name!

I thought, "How does that man know my name? No one but Jesus knows my name up here."

However, I found that everyone we met who talked to us knew my name. The conversations were just as they are on earth. People asked questions and answered them.

I looked up at the man in shock, but I answered him politely, as I had been taught, "Well, I'm doing okay."

And he invited us inside, so Jesus and I walked in and sat down. Now the couches in heaven are different than here. Earth furniture sometimes becomes uncomfortable. In heaven, comfort finds you. I sat down on a black velvet couch, and comfort reached up and cuddled me. I was so comfortable, I never had to move once.

After we finished talking, the man took us through the house. His mansion seemed just like houses on earth, but it was total perfection. The windows had curtains over them. The walls were decorated with paintings, which in this particular house, reminded me of modern art on earth, except better.

Also, there were photographs of the man's family members, and there were plants everywhere. In addition, the mansion was filled with beautiful furniture and luxuries. Some things I did not recognize.

Each mansion was suited to the person who lived there, for every child of God has his or her own mansion in heaven. (John 14:2.) This one had different rooms, such as dining room, living room, kitchen, den, and so forth. (I am sure there were bedrooms, but I did not go upstairs.)

The man gave me a large fruit to eat, that looked something like an apple, and it was very delicious. Afterwards, we said goodby and left through the back door. I cannot tell you why, but that is the way we went out. There were other people in the house, and they hugged and kissed us before we left.

Eating in heaven is something many people seem to have a problem with believing. Yet, the Apostle John wrote about the marriage supper of the Lamb. (Rev. 19:19.) Also, John wrote of seeing the tree of life which has 12 kinds of fruit that it yields every month. (Rev. 22:2.) In addition, Jesus ate fish and bread with the disciples *after* he was resurrected and had a transfigured body, the kind we will have in heaven. (Luke 24:42, John 21:9.)

Every person I saw looked in perfect condition and in the prime of life. Everyone appeared as if they were in their 30s. Perhaps that is because the Bible says we shall be like Him (1 John 3:2), and that was His age when He was resurrected and taken back to heaven. I did not see any children; however, somehow I knew there were children. Apparently, they were in another part, and I did not go there.

Also, I found that people's age is reckoned according to their spiritual maturity, not their physical maturity on earth. When you get to heaven, you will be the age you are spiritually in the hidden man of the heart.

Animals in Heaven

Jesus and I continued walking. As we went over a few hills, I noticed more things. I saw all kinds of animals, every kind you could think of, from A to Z. Sometimes people have questioned this, but if you think about it, why should there not be animals in heaven? The Bible talks about horses in heaven, so why would God only have one kind of animal?

The most well-known reference, of course, is to Jesus returning to earth on a white horse. (Rev. 19:11.) Also, horses and a chariot were sent from heaven after Elijah when he was taken up. (2 Kings 2:11,12.) Both chariot and horses looked like fire.

Some time after that, Elisha asked God to open the eyes of his servant to see that more troops were with Israel than with the enemy.

. . . And the Lord opened the eyes of the young man; and he saw: and, behold, the mountain was full of *horses* and chariots of fire round about Elisha.

2 Kings 6:17

I saw a dog, a baby goat, and a lion of great strength. There were birds singing in the trees, all sizes of birds, and they seemed to be singing the same song. After they stopped singing, it almost seemed as if they were talking among themselves!

There were other animals I saw at a distance, but I could not identify them. They neither ran from people nor tried to attack them, however. All were calm and peaceful. *Fear cannot be found in heaven.* God's presence is so strong that fear, confusion, doubt, sickness, and worry are not found there.

I also looked at the trees we passed. The leaves swayed back and forth, dancing and praising as we passed. You would have thought a great wind was blowing through the land. The grass was green, the very essence of green, and very soft. After we passed, the footprints in the grass sprang back into perfection, immediately erasing any footprints.

Many men will be happy to know that you never have to mow the lawn in heaven! The grass is always the same length. And, if a leaf falls, it disappears. There is no rotten fruit on the trees, because death and decay have no part in heaven. There is not one thing wrong and not one problem to be found.

Of course, no doubt and disbelief can be found there, because the Source of life is there. The goodness of God abounds in heaven.

3

The Cloud of Witnesses

Jesus and I became friends as He took me on a tour of heaven. I was very comfortable with Him and not a bit nervous about what I said or did. When I looked down at myself, I found I was dressed just like everyone else we met.

All of the saints whom I saw were dressed in white clothes — "white robes of righteousness."

> **And to her** (the Bride of Christ collectively and the saints of God individually) **was granted that she should be arrayed in fine linen, clean and white: for the fine linen is the righteousness of saints.**
>
> **Revelation 19:8**

Some of the people I saw wore jewelry, and others wore different colored sashes. Of course, no one was into vanity or pride in appearance, but apparently, even in heaven, God wants all of His children to do Him credit and look nice. The white linen robe, however, is the important part of heavenly apparel.

Since my visit to heaven, I have never understood people who seem to think they will do nothing but float lazily around on clouds when they reach the heavenly realm. If God does not approve of self-indulgence and idleness (Prov. 6:6, 15:19) on earth, He certainly is not going to allow it in heaven. There is no laziness in heaven — none at all.

I also get concerned at all the misinformation about angels that not only permeates the world, but the Church! You see pictures of cherubs three-feet-tall and half-naked, shooting bows and arrows of "love" at people. And there even was a recent popular television series based on the fallacy that people turn into angels after they die.

Even worse, that show and another very popular movie that surfaces around Christmas each year, *It's a Wonderful Life,* is built around the idea that people who want to become angels can *earn* their wings. Nothing in heaven is *earned* by "works of the flesh" — good or bad. All of it is a free gift from God the Father to His beloved children.

People need to understand that angels are completely different beings from mankind. Apparently, from records in the Bible, there are several different kinds of winged celestial beings.

Cherubim are awesome creatures, about as far from the fat little cherubs of romantic fiction that you could imagine. Then there are messenger angels, warrior angels, and seraphim. Probably, there are many other kinds that are not mentioned.

Cherubim technically are not classed as angels, but are a different order of being. They protected the Garden of Eden with flaming swords after Adam and Eve had been put out onto the earth to live. (Gen. 3:24.) Moses was told to make golden replicas of cherubims to shadow (Ex. 25:18; Heb. 9:5), or make a covering of glory, for the Ark of the Covenant.

Cherubs are called *living creatures* by Ezekiel in describing his vision of the abominations being carried out in the temple in Jerusalem. (Ezek. 10:20, 16:15.) He said the cherubims had four faces: the face of a cherub, the face of a man, the face of a lion, and the face of an eagle. (Ezek. 10:14, 20-22.)

In fact, in the passage in Ezekiel that commonly is considered to refer to Satan, he is called **the anointed cherub that covereth** (Ezek. 28:14). We usually call the devil a "fallen angel," but according to the Word, he was a far higher-level being than that. He actually was one of the awesome-looking cherubim — and the highest rank in heaven. When he rebelled, however, he was able to persuade a third of the angels in heaven to follow him. (Rev. 12:4.)

There are many accounts of angels in the Bible. Some came to bring judgment, as to Sodom and Gomorrah (Gen. 19); some brought warnings, such as the one with a drawn sword who appeared to Balaam (Num. 22:22-35); and some brought answers to prayer, like the one who came to Daniel after he had fasted twenty-one days. (Dan. 10:13.)

From my observations, angels are seven feet tall, and some are taller. They are fully dressed, according to the purpose and level of their assignment. Some have wings, and some of them do not.

Seraphims (Is. 6:2,26) have six wings, according to the prophet Isaiah. Truly, there are things in heaven more wonderful than we can ever imagine. (1 Cor. 2:9.)

That's the way I saw them.

A Service of Praise

Soon I saw a huge building resembling a convention center here on earth. Thousands of saints were going into it. The building had a glowing circle around it.

Jesus and I were met by two angels who escorted us down to the second row, where two seats were reserved. People greeted us on the way down to our seats. There was not a sad face in the entire place.

You would have thought we were at a family reunion where people had not seen one another in years. They were hugging and kissing each other, and saying, ''How are you? Glory to God!'' They seemed to be permeated with an attitude of love. They loved everybody. They did not care what you looked like or where you were from, they just loved you. Everything they did was out of a motive of love.

As soon as we were seated, a holy hush swept over the entire auditorium. You literally could have heard a pin drop. From the right of the stage, 500 to 600 praisers walked out. These were people, not angels.

They were dressed similarly to a church choir on earth. They wore robes, and everything about them was absolute perfection. These saints were smiling as they walked out on stage. All of a sudden, they began to praise God and lost all resemblance to a formal choir.

Their hands went up, their voices lifted in praise songs, and they began to dance. The service was not comparable to our praise services on earth. The audience joined in, not ashamed to praise God, either. Everyone lifted their hands, praised God, and jumped up and down. The service seemed to last about two hours.

No one led, but everyone moved in unison. In spite of the singing and dancing, everything was done in perfect order — everything. There was never a dead space of silence. The praise never died down, but grew in power and momentum. When I looked over at Jesus, He was smiling widely and obviously enjoying the service.

One observation regarding our services on earth is that we let praise die down too soon. We do not keep going. We have not yet learned the sacrifice of praise and worship. To *really* praise God, we need to cross the line in the spirit where joy becomes evident in our praise. If we do that, I believe we will see signs and wonders.

Praise is a substance. I saw all of the praises ascend out of the mouths of the people as glowing, bright vapors that collected at the top of the building. When the service was complete, the collected praise shot out of the top of the building and went to the Throne Room of God.

The writer of the books of Chronicles described this kind of praise that took place when Solomon dedicated the house he had made for God in Jerusalem.

(. . . Also the Levites which were the singers . . . arrayed in white linen, having cymbals and psalteries and harps, stood at the east end of the altar, and with them an hundred and twenty priests sounding with trumpets:)

It came even to pass, as the trumpeters and singers were *as one,* to make *one* sound to be heard in praising and thanking the Lord; and when they lifted up their voice with the trumpets and cymbals and instruments of music, and praised the Lord, saying, For he is good; for his mercy endureth for ever: that then the house was filled with a cloud, even the house of the Lord.

2 Chronicles 5:12,13

In worship, miracles occur. Sometimes they will occur during praise, but when a congregation moves into true worship, I believe miracles will occur. I have seen many miracles occur during my ministry as we worshipped God, when everyone present was giving his or her all to God. You must not hold back. You must give everything you have to God, in order to receive everything He has to give you in return.

Those saints I saw in heaven gave 100 percent to everything they did. They were greatly enjoying the service and said afterwards they could not wait for the next one. Praising God is going to be a large part of our lives when we get to heaven.

Jesus asked me, "How did you like the service?"

I said, "I loved it!"

Tears of Intercession

We left the building, and as we walked along, Jesus began to cry. I was astounded. Jesus the Christ, the Son of God, began to cry! He turned toward me, shedding tears of intercession. Some things are too sacred to repeat, but this one thing He told me I could tell:

"Roberts, I love my people so much that I would go back to earth, preach my three years over again, and die for just *one* person. If I had not already paid the price for them, and if I thought they wanted to come to heaven, I would do it all over again.

"I would not have to know they would make it. If I just thought they *wanted* to come, I would do it for them, even if they were the greatest sinner of all."

He kept saying, "I love my people so much. Why do people not take Me at My Word? Do they not know that I have all power in heaven and on earth to back up what I said? It is so easy. I made it so simple. If people would just take Me at My Word, I will do what I said."

Then He cried harder and said, "I do not understand why people say they believe I will do something, but when it does not happen in their time, they begin to doubt my Word. If they will just believe and say with confidence that I will do it, I *will* do it at the correct time."

I knew Jesus was crying because of our unbelief. I was only eight years old, but I knew what unbelief was and how it hurt Jesus. I made a covenant with Jesus right then never to doubt His words and to let God be God. Now, when I am about to think or say something in doubt, I remember the tears of intercession that fell from Jesus' eyes, and I put off any doubt and unbelief.

When we came to a branch of the River of Life, we took off our shoes and got in. The water was knee-deep and crystal clear. Do you know the first thing Jesus did to me? He dunked me! I got back up and splashed Him, and we had a water fight. We splashed each other and laughed. We walked on the inside of the water. I know you will not be able to understand that, and I do not either, really. But that is what we did.

That meant something to me, for the King of Glory, the Son of God, to take time out for little eight-year-old Roberts, to play with him in the River of Life. When I get back to heaven, I want to put up a historical marker on that spot that will say: This spot is where Jesus Christ became not only Roberts Liardon's Lord and Savior, but his friend.

Yes, He became my friend. Now we walk and talk together. When I hear a good joke, I can run to Jesus and hear Him laugh at it. And when He gets a good one, He tells me. You know, God has some jokes He will tell you, if you are sensitive enough to hear His voice. His jokes are *very* funny and never boring. After all, the Bible does tell us that God laughs. (Ps. 2:4, Ps. 37:13.)

The River of Life is quite different from anything on earth. When you walk into it, it purifies you. It cleanses you of anything remaining from your earthlife and gives you life from its source, the Throne Room of God. (Rev. 22:1,2.)

The River of Life flows like a mountain stream, and there is no bottom to it. It is crystal clear all the way through. After we had played in it for a while, we got out. Then what felt like a huge hair dryer blew by and dried our clothes instantly. We put on our shoes and left.

Our "Family" Cheers Us On

Then we passed something I never, ever expected to see in heaven, something that struck me as the funniest thing I had ever seen. Yet, when I understood, it was the most encouraging and moving thing I perhaps have yet seen in my Christian walk.

Hebrews 12:1 talks of a "great cloud of witnesses":

> **Wherefore seeing we also are compassed about with so great a cloud of witnesses, let us lay aside every**

**weight, and the sin which doth so easily best us, and
let us run with patience the race that is set before us.**

I *saw* that great cloud of witnesses. *They are aware of what
the Church is doing spiritually.* When I am preaching, for
example, they are cheering me on, yelling, "Do this, do that,
go!" When "half time" comes, every one of them hits his
knees and begins to pray. Half time is prayer time. Then
they get back up and start cheering again.

It is as though we are in a big game, one that is serious
and very real, not a game for fun. And we have some fans
who are cheering us on. They are backing us 100 percent,
saying, "Go! Go get 'em! That's right! Go!"

If we could clearly understand the scripture about there
being one family in heaven and earth, we could hear in our
spirits what the part of our family in heaven is saying. If
we could hear the cloud of witnesses, we would be
successful in every area of our lives. To do this, you simply
have to get over into the realm of the spirit.

People ask me from time to time about real family
members who have passed on: "Will I see my cousin when
I get to heaven, and will I know him?" I truly believe that
in God's sight, the importance of our "spiritual family"
outweighs that of our natural family. Even though you will
recognize your cousin once you get to heaven, you might
be surprised to discover that the relationships you place the
most importance on in heaven are the ones with the people
God has placed in your "spiritual family," not necessarily
your "natural family."

4
Unclaimed Blessings

The next thing I saw on my tour was another building, but this one was very large and strange-looking. I became very curious about this building, because lightning was bolting in and out of it, and I heard rumblings and thunder from within.

Usually, I asked questions of Jesus in an audible voice, and He answered me audibly.

But this time, I just thought, "I wonder what that building is," and His answer came to me immediately.

"It is the Throne Room of God."

Another unique thing about this building was the seven rows of flowers in the front. They lined the pathway up to the door. Everything in heaven has a purpose, and seven is the number used in the Bible to symbolize perfection and completeness.[1] The colors of the flowers changed constantly into all of the colors of the rainbow. Every flower, bud, and leaf was uniform in size.

Also, in front of this building were 12 trees — not trees that we know on earth, but heaven's trees. There was the tree of wisdom that bears the fruit of wisdom, the tree of love that bears the fruit of love, and so forth. There was the tree of life that bears 12 kinds of fruit and its leaves "heal" nations. *Twelve* is the number of divine government.[2]

---

[1]Conner, Kevin J. *Interpreting the Symbols and Types* (Portland: Bible Temple Publishing, 1980), p. 6.

[2]Ibid, p. 7.

> And he shewed me a pure river of water of life, clear as crystal, proceeding out of the throne of God and of the Lamb.
>
> In the midst of the street of it, and on either side of the river, was there the tree of life, which bare twelve manner of fruits, and yielded her fruit every month: and the leaves of the tree were for the healing of the nations.
>
> **Revelation 22:1,2**

And I saw two warrior angels standing in front of the door. Each held a sword, and the blades of these swords were flames of fire. These two angels always stand outside the Throne Room with their flaming swords fully lit.

The Storehouses of Heaven

We walked a little farther — and *this is the most important, and perhaps the strangest, part of my story.* I saw three storage houses 500 to 600 yards from the Throne Room of God. They were very long and very wide. There may be more, but I only saw three. We walked into the first. As Jesus shut the front door behind us, I looked around the interior in shock!

On one side of the building were exterior parts of the body. Legs hung from the wall, but the scene looked natural, not grotesque. On the other side of the building were shelves filled with eyes: green ones, brown ones, blue ones, and so forth.

This building contained all of the parts of the human body that people on earth need, but Christians have not realized these blessings are waiting in heaven. There is no place else in the universe for these parts to go except right here on earth; no one else needs them.

Jesus said to me, "These are the unclaimed blessings. This building should not be full. It should be emptied. You should come in here with faith and get the needed parts for you, and the people you will come in contact with that day.''

The unclaimed blessings are there in those storehouses — all of the parts of the body people might need: hundreds of new eyes, legs, skin, hair, eardrums — they are all there. All you have to do is go in and get what you need by the arm of faith, because it is there.

You do not have to cry and beg God to *make* the part you need. Just go *get* it. The doors to the storehouses are never locked. They are always open for those who need to go in. We should empty those buildings.

Sometimes when we pray, an angel will leave heaven to bring us the answer — just as the angel did for Daniel (Dan. 10:12) but can't get through right away. Daniel kept praying and fasting for 21 days, until he got his answer. Because of his persistence in prayer, the angel was able to get through the demonic hindrances of the second heavens, where the principalities, powers, and rulers of darkness of this world live. (Eph. 6:12.)

What would have happened if Daniel had not kept praying and ''pressing in'' to God for his answer? The angel might not have gotten through the warfare with the Prince of Persia (Dan. 10:13), and Daniel would not have received an answer.

If he were like many Christians today, he would have said, ''Well, this stuff just doesn't work. I prayed and fasted, and God didn't answer.''

But the truth is that he would not have gotten his answer because he quit; he gave up too soon.

Jesus *Wants* Us Healed and Whole

Because of my visit to heaven, I never had any doubt that Jesus not only wants His people well and whole but that healing is available for any who will receive. I knew beyond the shadow of a doubt that God did not put sickness and disease on people. I saw no sickness and disease in heaven during my visit, only provision for creative miracles.

Everything God gives us, made for us, or provided for us has its source in Himself and His heavenly Kingdom. So how could He give us sickness and disease when it is a purely earthly phenomenon, a result of the fall of Adam and Eve? Sickness, disease, lack of anything, and all the other woes of earth come from Satan, the father of lies and cause of death and destruction.

However, I do not base my knowledge of Jesus' provision for healing on my experience in heaven. I base it on the Word of God. There are many good books available on healing and no space in this one to deal with it in detail. But I do want to give two scriptures that prove healing is ours, for the benefit of readers who may not know this or may have been taught doctrines that say otherwise.

> **But he was wounded for our transgressions, he was bruised for our iniquities: the chastisement of our peace was upon him; and with his stripes we *are* healed.**
>
> **Isaiah 53:5**

That was a prophetic utterance made by the prophet looking forward to the time when Jesus would come to earth as the Messiah and go to the cross for mankind.

> **Who his own self bare our sins in his own body on the tree, that we, being dead to sins, should live unto righteousness: by whose stripes ye *were* healed.**
>
> **1 Peter 2:24**

The Apostle Peter quoted Isaiah, but changed the verb. Isaiah looked to the future; Peter used a past-tense verb. Isaiah looked forward to the coming of Jesus with healing in His wings (Mal. 4:2), and Peter said, ''It is already done! He *has* come with healing in His wings.''

Jesus wants us to be physically well for two reasons: He loves us and does not want us to be in pain, and He wants us to be able to do His will in ministry or in our lives without hindrances. Sickness and disease keep your mind on yourself rather than on others, drain finances that could be used in the Lord's work, and give Satan that much victory in your life.

Another doctrine that has been much taught is that God uses sickness and disease "to teach us a lesson." That is totally unscriptural. Would you put measles or smallpox on your child to "teach them a lesson"? If so, you would be a child abuser. And that is what God would be if He disciplined us with sickness and disease.

Jesus pointed out that if earthly fathers give their children good things, how much more will our Father in heaven give us, His children, good things. He said that if your child asked you for a fish, would you give him a snake? (Matt. 10:16; Luke 11:11.) Then why do people think God would do that?

If under the Old Covenant, God kept more than three million Hebrews well and free from disease, how much more will He keep His children under the New Covenant, which is a *better* covenant, well and free from disease? (Heb. 8:6.)

Look at Exodus 15:26:

> **If thou wilt diligently hearken to the voice of the Lord thy God, and wilt do that which is right in his sight, and wilt give ear to his commandments, and keep all his statutes, I will put none of these diseases upon thee, which I have brought upon the Egyptians: for *I am the Lord that healeth thee.***

Note that the condition to staying out from under the diseases was to **hearken to the voice** of God, **do that which is right in his sight,** and to **give ear to his commandments**

and keep all his statutes. To summarize: God was saying, ''If you will hear and obey Me, I can do this for you.''

Also, the Hebrew literally reads, ''I will *permit* none of these diseases upon thee which I *permitted* upon the Egyptians.''[3]

I did not know all these things when I visited heaven, but I learned them from God's Word as I grew up. But I *knew* after my visit that it is always the will of God to heal everyone who will hear and obey — which under the New Covenant means walking in love of God and your ''neighbor'' (Matt. 22:37-39) and faith. (Heb. 11.)

> **Therefore I say unto you, What things soever ye desire, when ye pray, believe that ye receive them, and ye shall have them.**
>
> **Mark 11:24**
>
> **But let him ask in faith, nothing wavering. For he that wavereth is like a wave of the sea driven with the wind and tossed.**
>
> **For let not that man think that he shall receive any thing of the Lord.**
>
> **A double-minded man is unstable in all his ways.**
>
> **James 1:6-8**

Even before this visit to heaven, as long as I can remember, I have believed that God's Word is true.

After Jesus showed me the Throne Room of God and the place where all of the unclaimed blessings are kept, we walked on a while and were quiet. I was thinking over everything I had seen and content just to be in the presence of Jesus.

Then Jesus began to tell me what He had called me to do as my life's work on earth.

---

[3]Osborn, T. L. *Healing the Sick, A Living Classic* (Tulsa: Harrison House, Inc., 1959), p. 23.

5

Jesus Ordained Me

Jesus took both my hands in one of His, and placed His other hand on top of my head.

He said, "Roberts, I am calling you to a great work. I am ordaining you to a great work. You will have to run like no one else and preach like no one else. You will have to be different from everyone else."

In other words, He was telling me not to copy others, not to try to fit into religious attitudes and patterns, but simply to do and be only what He wanted.

"Hard times will come," He warned me, "but take them as stepping stones, not as stumbling blocks. Go with power and with faith. I will be beside you wherever you go. Go, go, go! Go and do as I have done."

The first time Jesus said, "Go," the anointing and the fire began to flow from Him into me. That fire went from the top of my head to the soles of my feet. Now, every time I talk about God, whether it is to one or 3,000, I am set afire all over, such as Luke 3:16 says:

> **John answered, saying unto them all, I indeed baptize you with water; but one mightier than I cometh, the latchet of whose shoes I am not worthy to unloose: he shall baptize you with the Holy Ghost *and with fire*.**

The Church needs to get within the fire of God. That is what burns out all of the chaff in your life. Hebrews 12:29 says:

For our God is a consuming fire.

If you will let the fire of the Holy Spirit shoot through your body and make you pure, you will be able to walk before God boldly with a clean heart and a clean mind. You will know you can walk into His presence where you belong without being destroyed by His glory.

After praying for me and ordaining me, Jesus took a step backwards. I looked down at the palms of my hands. They were as red as blood.

As Jesus stepped back from me, he pulled down a big screen out of the air. On this screen He began to show me my past life.

At eight years of age, I did not have much of a past life, of course.

When Jesus began to show me my ministry and the people who would be saved through it, however, I did not want to miss reaching a single one of them — even if it *does* mean living to be an old man.

A greater miracle than even raising Lazarus from the dead is the miracle that occurs when someone is born again, raised from spiritual death and rescued from eternal damnation.

I saw myself preaching in various places.

Then I knew it was time to go.

I was turning to leave through the nearest gate, when Jesus said, "Roberts!" And I turned back very quickly. There stood Jesus with tears coming down His face and His hands outstretched.

He said, "I love you."

When He said that, I left heaven and returned to my earthly home.

Back on Earth

Of course, I was startled and I laid on my bed wondering about everything I had just experienced. I realized the experience had been real, because the fire and anointing continued to flow in me for several hours after I came back.

My trip to heaven had been so special that I cherished it close to me for a while. Then I was not sure that everyone would believe a little boy could be taken to heaven for a tour with Jesus. So it was about eight more years before I ever told about this experience.

I have always sensed that I was a type of forerunner for the young people God is going to use in this generation. In my ministry, I challenge the older people, but I identify with the young people.

My life and ministry, I believe, are examples of what God can do with you *if you will pay the price*. The price is total commitment, being totally sold out to the will of God. The price is praying each day and studying the Word. The price is putting Jesus absolutely before everything else.

First, you must choose whom you are going to serve. You will have to give up everything you have to God — everything from A to Z and beyond.

As I wrote earlier, Jesus and I are friends. We walk and talk together. We get on planes together. He sits down beside me. He does everything with me.

When I wake up in the morning, I say, "Good morning, Father. Good morning, Jesus. Good morning, Holy Spirit."

We cannot know the Trinity by our feelings. We learn to know them through the Word of God. Our emotions are fickle, because they have been influenced by the environment of the world and by the world's thinking. We cannot depend on our feelings. But if we study God's Word, we will learn to know God better.

God has a personality. He has emotions. He can be hurt because we have not talked to Him lately. I have found that God is three things: *light, life, and love.* God loves people so much that love boils up out of Him.

Abraham was called a friend of God. (James 2:23.) Daniel talked with God. You can be the friend of God also. When was the last time you said, "God, I love you?" Maybe that is overdue. Jesus wants us to be friends with Him. Many people who are His servants are not His friends. To be His friend requires obedience (John 15:14,15).

He wants to know you. He will meet you more than halfway. All you need to do is sit down and say, "God, I want to talk to you."

Jesus cares. If He did not care, He would not have died for you. He cares about everything — your lifestyle, your welfare. He cares and cares and cares.

The Holy Spirit wants to do something for you. He has a very colorful personality, of which most Christians are not aware. He is the One who makes you laugh and dance in the Spirit. He is the One who causes people to fall down (be "slain in the Spirit"), and He is the One who glues people to the floor so they cannot get up.

The Holy Spirit is the One who opens blind eyes and takes spiritual blinders off. He is the One who shows you things. *He is the power on earth of the Trinity.* He is the One who lives on the inside of us.

If we could realize that the *same power* that raised Jesus from the dead dwells in us, none of us would remain sick.

We need to learn to walk and talk with God as Enoch did. We need to get to know God for what He is, not for what His benefits are. If your heart is right toward God, *then* you will receive the benefits.

God is a big God, and He can take care of our little problems. As Smith Wigglesworth said, we must look at earth's problems from heaven's viewpoint.

God is alive and well, and He sits upon His Throne!

Other Visits From Jesus

Another time I saw Jesus, I was about 11 years old. This time, He walked in through the front door while I was watching the comedy, "Laverne and Shirley" on television. He came over, sat down beside me on the couch, and kind of glanced at the TV set.

Everything in this natural world clicked off. I could not hear the television or the telephone. All I heard was Jesus, and all I saw was His glory.

He said, "Roberts, I want you to study the lives of My generals in My great army throughout time. Know them like the back of your hand. Know why they were a success. Know why they failed, and you will lack nothing in that area."

Jesus promised me certain things that day.

He said, "Roberts, if you will be faithful in this thing, I will promote you."

The Bible says you must be faithful first of all in small things. (Matt. 25:21-23.)

I had to leave the television set alone after that. I had to turn my back on school sports. I had to leave everything, even my best friend, and do what was required of me to follow God in order to fill the office He has for me.

He made me another promise that day. He said that if I would be faithful in these studies, He would see that I met the great generals of this day. And God has kept His promise. He has brought me in contact with them. If you let God do it, things will happen in His time. Everything will work out all right — everything. For God has a timetable that He runs on. We need to run on His timetable.

Jesus got up, walked back out the door, the TV clicked back on, and I resumed watching — for that day, anyway.

After that, I studied carefully the great ministers of the past, along with some who were not well-known, to find out why they succeeded or failed. I began by reading a book my grandmother had on British evangelist Smith Wigglesworth.

Then I studied the lives and ministries of such men and women as John Alexander Dowie, Charles Finney, Maria Woodworth-Etter, John G. Lake, Aimee Semple McPherson, Kathryn Kuhlman, and many others.

Most of the time, we are running *from* the devil. But I found that the great preachers of the past lived on the offensive. They were not afraid of anything. We can learn much from the examples of these great men and women, who are now with the Lord.

As I read a book during those years I was studying what Jesus told me to study, the Holy Spirit taught me. He would tell me what different people were like.

He would say, "Did you notice that? Did you notice how they said that — how they moved with Me in this way?"

Looking Into Heaven

In January 1983, I was awakened by an angel at 5 a.m.

The angel said, "Look!" And I looked into heaven. This was a spiritual vision.

There is a difference between leaving your body and going to heaven and *looking* into heaven. I did not go back this time, I only looked.

Heaven sits on top of the universe — you have to go that far to reach it. You see, the universe is expanding at the same rate God spoke it into existence, and *the universe begins outside of heaven's gates.*

As I looked into heaven, I recognized the place where I had seen tens of thousands of chariots when I was 8 years old. Although these chariots probably were drawn by horses, I did not see the horses.

I turned around and asked Jesus, "What does this mean? Why did You notify me? Why did You have the angel show me this?"

"Remember the covenant you made with Me?" (While in heaven the first time, we had made a covenant.) "This is My part, so I am showing you that the chariots are gone. They have gone to earth and brought the power.

"The next move of God has arrived on planet earth. You no longer have to pray for it to happen. It has arrived!"

So people no longer have to say, "I am praying for the next move of God to happen."

We are in it! We are in it! We are in the moving of God for this hour of time, and we are just beginning to realize it is here.

As an historian of the Pentecostal movement, I have noticed that each time there was a move of God, new "weapons" always were released first.

The Church Is in Transition

This is a special time in Church history: I believe we are seeing the beginning of perhaps the final move of God. This move is going to be a storm of the Spirit. The glory clouds will roll in. The lightnings of God are going to hit.

The former and latter rain will be falling at the same time, and the winds and thunders of God will be heard. That is a storm in the Spirit, and it is going to happen — you just wait and see. Those who doubt what the Holy Spirit is doing will be washed away in the flood.

God will use those who are willing and those who will yield to His power. He cannot wait any longer for man to get ready. He will take whoever is willing, whether they are 96 or two years old. I advise everyone to get willing, so the power of God can flow through you. Get ready to be used; otherwise, you are going to be left behind.

The Church is in a transition period right now. We have been changing gears to overdrive during the past decade. In the '90s, we are going to see more of the miraculous. In fact, the miracles we will see will seem almost unbelievable.

Healings are gradual, and miracles are instantaneous. We have seen a lot of healings, and healings are important. There will still be healings, but we will see more miracles: blind eyes opened, cripples healed, missing legs restored instantly.

The day will come when every single person in a meeting will be healed. This move of the Holy Spirit will be the demonstration of the power of God.

Another thing that will happen is that *the mantles of great men and prophets will fall on individuals who can handle the responsibility.* The mantles of Jeremiah, Isaiah, and other people in the New Testament — even throughout history — will start to fall on people. These believers will operate in the power of that past individual's mantle, as well as under their own mantles.

Not everyone, however, is going to get a mantle — understand that. God has reserved these mantles for this end time, because this is going to be the *greatest* outpouring of the Holy Spirit the world has ever seen.

The mysterious things of God are all around us just waiting to be discovered. Begin doing spiritual exploring and experimenting to understand how the mysteries of God work. Stir up the gifts of the Spirit. (2 Tim. 1:6.)

During this move, the Church is going to destroy the kingdom of darkness. And prayer warriors have a tremendous role to play.

One example of the power of God demonstrated in action occurred in Tulsa, Oklahoma, once when I was preaching to about 250 young people.

As I started to minister with the laying on of hands, the lightnings of God started hitting the people. Sinners and saints alike saw the lightnings of God come out of my fingers and hit the people.

And the oddest thing happened: I forgot to give an altar call! But sinners were so astounded and moved that they began to hunt people in the congregation who knew God.

Some young people ran to the pastor and to me, asking, "How do we get to God? How? How?"

When the power of God is in demonstration, you do not have to give an altar call. Sinners will hunt God without an invitation from you. The power of God was so strong in the auditorium that night that people standing within six feet of the platform started to fall, even those who consciously resisted.

Young people who would not cry before their parents began to cry before the whole audience.

The Holy Spirit Is Always Moving

Many times we wait for the Holy Spirit to move and wonder why He is not moving. We talk about "moves" of the Spirit. Yet, He *always is moving*. The gifts of the Spirit are already in operation. The problem is that we do not move into the realm of the spirit where the gifts are.

When you get into the place in the spirit where you are near the Holy Spirit, signs and wonders will follow you. You will become numb to this world and to people's criticism. All of the things that fascinate your natural body will fall away, and everything will be in tune with God.

Your body is not *you*. You are a spirit who lives in a body and has a soul — mind, will, and emotions. You need to bring your soul and body under the authority of the real you, the spirit being.

If your spirit, soul, and body are in the proper order, you will not need to seek a prophecy from the Lord or visions from God to know what to do. It is good to have a leading from the Spirit, but those supernatural occurrences are part of a teaching process, I believe.

I work toward the day when I will be so in tune with God that He will just *think,* and I *will* know what to do. That is the way it should be.

Prophets operated that way in Bible days. Many times, they just *knew* what needed to be done, and they just went and did it.

For example, when Elijah raised the widow's son from the dead (1 Kings 17:17-24), he did not have a vision, sign, or wonder from the Lord.

Elijah simply said, **O Lord my God, I pray thee, let this child's soul come into him again** (1 Kings 17:21).

And the child came back to life and was restored to his mother, who said: **Now by this I *know* that thou art a man of God, and that the word of the Lord in thy mouth is truth** (1 Kings 17:24a).

That is where we need to be — close enough to God that when He thinks, we know what to do without His having to tell us, ''Go pray for that individual. Go do this or that.''

Also, the way God does everything is *now*. You see, in heaven there is neither past nor future. Everything is in the present. *Now* is the day of salvation. *Now* you are healed. *Now, now, now.*

We are conditioned to walk in the time of this realm, but when we get over into the realm of the Spirit, we walk outside of time. Time is peculiar to earth. For this move of God to be successful, we must get to the point of walking and talking with God as a friend and seeing things from His viewpoint. We must not be locked in to tradition, to time, or to the world's opinions.

6

Heaven Can Be *Your* Destination

There is a real, literal heaven. Only thirteen books in the Bible do not mention heaven, and even in those, the principles and concepts are in line with the idea of a literal place called heaven.

Heaven is first of all the place where God lives. Yet it is not enough to contain Him, as King Solomon knew when he built the first temple for God on earth.

But will God indeed dwell on the earth? behold, the heaven and heaven of heavens cannot contain thee; how much less this house that I have builded?

1 Kings 8:27

As I wrote earlier, things on earth are shadows of heavenly things. Moses was given the details of the tabernacle to be built in the wilderness (the forerunner of the later temple) and told that it was patterned on a heavenly tabernacle, which God had built.

Who serve unto the example and shadow of heavenly things, as Moses was admonished of God when he was about to make the tabernacle: for, See, saith he, that thou make all things according to the pattern shewed to thee in the mount.

Hebrews 8:5

. . . We have such an high priest, who is set on the right hand of the throne of the Majesty in the heavens:

A minister of the sanctuary, and of the true tabernacle, which the Lord pitched, and not man.

Hebrews 8:1,2

Psalm 102:19 says that the Lord looks down on the earth from **the height of his sanctuary; from heaven did the Lord behold the earth.** *Heaven* is so taken for granted as the place where God lives that writers of the books of the Bible, under inspiration of the Holy Spirit, often use *heaven* and *God* interchangeably. In Luke 15:18, the Prodigal Son said **I have sinned against heaven** (God).

The things I saw in heaven may not be the things described by someone else who had the privilege of visiting there and returning. That is because heaven is a gigantic place, and all of it is not shown to any one person anymore than a visitor to the United States could tell you what the East, North, South, West, Southwest, Midwest, and so forth were all like.

The important thing is that God is real, He lives in a real place, and we will be in a real place when we arrive at His home. We will have bodies that are perfect, never grow old, and never get sick. They will be made of whatever material the supernatural realm consists of, just as our natural bodies were created by God from the dust of the ground of this earth.

You have already seen that people walk, talk, have houses, and eat in heaven — not just from my vision, but from scriptures I have quoted in this book. You have seen there are lands, streets, towns, country, rivers, and streams. There are flowers and trees, animals and birds.

Unbelievers, you *already* have eternal life. No spirit being apparently can ever disappear out of existence (die), according to the Bible. What is in question, however, is *where* will you live the rest of your life? Where will you spend the endless days and nights, after this short span of time — like snapping your fingers compared to eternity — is over?

Would you like to know that your final destination was the habitation of God?

Would you like to be "raised from the dead" (spiritually) and literally become a new creature in the image of Jesus? (2 Cor. 5:17.)

Would you like to be able to have victory over Satan on earth and then live on victorious, active and happy, working for God throughout all eternity?

If you want these things, you can have them.

If you want Jesus to come into your heart and be the Lord of your life, He will.

Romans 10:9,10 says:

If thou shalt confess with thy mouth the Lord Jesus, and shalt believe in thine heart that God hath raised him from the dead, thou shalt be saved.

For with the heart man believeth unto righteousness; and with the mouth confession is made unto salvation.

If you want this salvation and assurance of living eternally with the Creator of the universe, pray this prayer:

Lord, forgive me of my sins. You said if we were quick to confess our sins, You would be faithful to forgive. (1 John 1:9) You sent Your only begotten Son to die on the cross at Calvary almost 2,000 years ago because You loved us so much. (John 3:16) So I know that if I ask Jesus into my heart — as I do right now — He will come in and live with me.

Jesus, I do receive You as my Savior, Healer, Deliverer, High Priest, and Lord. You are King of kings and Lord of lords, and I want to give my life to you as You gave your life for me. I want You to be my best Friend forever, and I will serve you all of the days of this life and throughout eternity.

Now that you have made this decision, find a local church where they believe and teach the full gospel, one that believes the Bible is the inspired Word of God. You will need to tell the pastor that you have asked Christ into your heart and that you need to be baptized. (Mark 16:16.)

There is no substitute for fellowship in a local church and for being pastored by a man or woman who has a real heart for God's children under their care.

Get a version of the Bible that you feel comfortable with reading. Most towns of any size have Christian bookstores, and even shopping mall bookstore chains usually have a shelf with Bibles on it. The *King James Version* is the traditional English version, and many people still would rather read it. However, the *New International Version* is in today's English, as is the *New American Standard,* and some others.

For your first good, sound study Bible, you are better off with a *translation* rather than a *paraphrase* in modern language, of which there are several available. No matter how well-intentioned the authors are, any paraphrase is simply someone's opinion of what the *King James Version* means. A translation uses the English word that best *translates,* or is a counterpart, of a Hebrew or Greek word.

If you have made this decision, please write me at the address below. I want to send you some free literature to help you in your new walk with Jesus Christ.

Roberts Liardon Ministries
P. O. Box 30710
Laguna Hills, CA 92654
714-661-3606

Roberts Liardon was born in Tulsa, Oklahoma. He was born again, baptized in the Holy Spirit, and called to the ministry at the age of eight, after being caught up to Heaven by the Lord Jesus.

Roberts was powerfully commissioned by the Lord to study the lives of God's great "generals" — men and women of faith who were mightily used by God in the past — in order to learn why they succeeded and why they failed.

At age fourteen, Roberts began preaching and teaching in various churches — denominational and non-denominational alike — Bible colleges and universities. He has traveled extensively, in the United States and Canada, and his missions outreaches have taken him to Africa, Europe and Asia. Many of his books have been translated into foreign languages.

Roberts preaches and ministers under a powerful anointing of the Holy Spirit. In his sermons, Roberts calls people of all ages to salvation, holiness and life in the Holy Spirit.

Through Roberts' ministry around the world, many people have accepted God's call to yield themselves as vessels for the work of the Kingdom.